Going Home

Death . . . and Eden, After

Words of comfort for all who mourn
Words of acceptance for family and friends
Words of insight for any needing and able to hear

CHARLES A. WILKINSON

FolioAvenue Publishing Service
2031 Union Street, Suite 6,
San Francisco CA 94123 415-869-8834
(866-365-4628) www.folioavenue.com

ISBN: Paperback: 978-1-951193-59-1
          Hardback: 978-1-951193-60-7

Dedication

To those who have gone before
but remain forever
within my heart and soul

*Dying will have its way with all of us
while death awaits to embrace and welcome us home*

A Word Before...

All that follows is framed by Teilhard de Chardin, a Jesuit priest and scientist who wrote that "We are spiritual beings having a human experience." If that is so, the meaning of "home" for the purpose of these pages is "where we come from," or as Robert Frost said, "where, when you have to go there, they have to take you in." That being said, let's start at the beginning,

From somewhere in forever, where neither time nor place apply, eternal energy or spirit takes on the form we call human life. In that transition we all leave home, falling into humanness, to experience a journey like no other. We live searching for meaning and fulfillment, all the while sensing time, which we created, measuring our mortality. Still, the eternal energy of our spiritual being is at the heart of our journey, reminding us of the home we came from, all the while luring us back there.

On our journey our mortality tells us we are dying. At different times, with varying intensities, that realization renders us restless and anxious; we need to make our journey meaningful before our return. Dag Hammarskjold wrote in his book *Markings,* "Do not seek death. Death will find you. But seek that road which makes death a fulfillment."

Life itself, both fragile and precious, needs an explanation, a fulfillment. And so we turn to God, or the Uncaused Cause, or Love - that is, whatever is eternal and can explain the energy in the Universe, in all of creation.

If Chardin's insight rings true, death is the welcoming home embrace at the end of the journey. It is the dying that is the hard part.

"We are born from a quiet sleep and we die to a calm awakening."

- Zhuangzi

Death, My Friend

Death, my friend,
tell Dying to be kind to me
if only because you sense my gratitude
for the grace of life,
for breath and time and, ah,
the touch of an other's heart.

> *Tell Dying to be kind*
> *when it comes calling;*
> *just not too soon.*

Let me know you know my name
and how I have loved - or tried to,
seeking a wholeness
you will find me still reaching for.

> *Come while I am dreaming*
> *or in the midst of laughter.*
> *But come with gentle certainty,*
> *please, my friend.*

Don't let my dying
take me piece by piece
but all, at once,
assuring me in your embrace
that there is something more than time;
and someone waiting,
waiting in the Now
that is our forever home.

There is a difference between dying and death itself. Dying takes on many forms, is measured by time, can be a sudden or long term, kind or cruel. Death is simply the end of all of that. The last body-collapsing breath, the flat, dull eyes, the almost instant coolness and opaqueness of the skin. Death is the end of human living. Energy, spirit-self moves on. Dying, however it happens, becomes an inevitable part of everyone's story and journey through time.

I take comfort in the story of a priest-friend who, while golfing said, "I didn't know angels were allowed on golf courses. There's been one following us for the last few holes." His buddies shrugged his comment off as his kind of joke until he said at the next tee, "There's that angel again and, hey, it's coming toward us." Then, he dropped dead, just like that! It was as if, for him, death, though far from timely, came calling in a kindly way to take him home.

"Death is nothing else but going home to God, the bond of love will be unbroken for all eternity."

- Mother Teresa

Death and Reality

Death seems always to happen to other people. What is it inside us that denies it will happen to us? Maybe the power of living is so all involving that we just do not choose to give death a purchase with us, at least until we have no choice about it.

I still remember my twin brother's dying. He never seemed to let the idea in, even in his final conscious moments. He just did not put words to his dying, as if doing so would give dying permission to have its way. He never said his thank you's and goodbye's like my sister did a few years earlier. She knew there was something more and was ready for it. It was as if she lived for years with death as a friend. My brother, it seemed, never let death into his thinking. I do not think he was afraid of it; just that he refused to see it as an option. He died saying a stubborn "No" while my sister died exhaling an accepting "Yes."

I treasure the gifts both siblings gave me in their dyings. I thank God I can say I have no fear of death though I readily admit being anxious about how I might die. I hope to die like my sister, full of gratitude and readiness, conscious and with the sense of loving and being loved. I want to feel finished with this part of the journey and curious about the next part. These wintering days I am thinking quite a bit about that. It is somehow comforting to try to make friends with death, which is what these thoughts are all about.

My hope is that they can help those who hear them to quell the fear of death itself and accept dying as the price of mortality.

When the Light Goes Out

When the light goes out
where will I be;
or was I already there?
I cannot know
until the darkness comes
and stillness claims
what remains of me.
Somehow an energy moves on
to claim the Now forever.

> *When the light goes out*
> *others reach for memories –*
> *the threads of life*
> *and the love they hold.*
> *Those left behind*
> *clutch with soft tears*
> *the darkness of loss,*
> *unwilling to let go of*
> *that piece of their hearts.*

When the light goes out
certainty and peace settle in,
for my Being
will become whole
...and holy.
There is no darkness
in the eternal Now; just love
that needs not eyes,
nor voice, nor even heart
to sigh the Amen
of being home.

"For life and death are one, even as the river and the sea are one."

- Khalil Gibran

It helps if one can feel they have lived a life with meaning, which also helps to face any fear of dying alone. I may be alone when death calls but I will not be without love and the presence of so many who live in my heart and bless my being, who in so many ways contribute to my life's meaning.

I have been told to live every day as though it is my last. I cannot do that, if only because I would go insane trying to get everything in place and miss the gift of time itself in the process. So I try to live every day as a gift and am finding an energy at this stage of life that is both surprising and renewing. I would like to think I am ready to go and in a way I am. But I am feeling there is still much to be done, whatever that means, so I am grateful for every sunrise.

Still, I am very aware of the fragility of life these time-thin days - that is, the possibility of a debilitating disease, a stroke, a fall or dementia and the loss of dignity; and having to impose my helpless self on others. Some or all of that may be ahead but I pray not. In the meantime, I thank God for this gift of time.

Someone asked recently, "When is 'bonus time' for you? Are you in it yet?" I thought of extra innings, overtime or stoppage time in soccer and said I don't want to think I am there yet. Maybe I am but I don't want to have to watch the clock, just take each day as a gift and make the most of it.

Death is a given - for all of us. In an instant the light goes out and we are gone - and suddenly and eternally home. Many live with the belief that there is something more, something whole and holy, that there in an afterlife. That kind of faith can render the fear of death powerless...and the transition at least acceptable.

Dying is another matter altogether. It is too easily said that we are, all of us, dying from the moment of our conception. Though there is truth in that, most choose to live "into life" and all of its challenges and surprises. Death, even for those in denial, is a reality only for others, not for a self in the fullness of being and becoming.

Despite the capacity of the human body to endure, life is as fragile as the finest porcelain, the thinnest Irish Belleek. Time and fate have all of us living at risk and, though few of us can know when we will die, it is the how of dying that disturbs the edges of aging's consciousness. Some, tragically, solve that uneasiness by suicide, claiming a tragic kind of power over their dying. Others wish and pray for a peaceful dying - in their sleep, or a sudden and final heart attack or aneurysm that spares others the burden of their incapacities.

When, upon a certain age or circumstance, death becomes a hovering companion or a shadowy presence in our lives, it might help to stop, turn to death and ask, "Can we talk?" I cannot speak for others but I find that doing so, putting words to feelings, is quite helpful and far from morbid.

Naming my fears of how I am going to die will not in any way short-circuit the process but may calm my spirit-self facing the inevitability of death and the finiteness of my humanness.

The reality of death all around me lets me
know that in dying, most simply said:

- *I would rather not;*
- *I wish not to suffer;*
- *I do not want to be alone or, rather, not die lonely;*
- *I want to be aware of my going, to be able to say
  "Goodbye" and "Thank you."*
- *I want to die believing;*
- *I want to be grateful for all I have been given,
  especially love;*
- *I want to be forgiven;*
- *I want to be celebrated, not mourned;*
- *I want to be remembered kindly, and missed, as I
  miss those who have gone ahead;*
- *I want to be fulfilled in my faith;*
- *I would like to feel finished; and*
- *I want to be surprised on the other side.*

There is nothing original or unique in any of the above,
only the voice, but a fellow can wish, can't he?

Between now and then there is much to be done. Death's
shadowy presence has become something familiar,
reminding me of time passing, not to leave anything
important undone, to make the most of the moment and,
God willing, the years ahead.

Not surprisingly, every so often, it is Death, not I, who
asks, "Can we talk?"

"People living deeply have no fear of death."

- Anais Nin

Life and Death

It is Life that can be cruel, not Death;
Life - and Time that renders every life fragile.
Any moment can obliterate dreams,
leaving human love
to bleed both loss and sorrow.
It is Life that does so, not Death.
Death is a kindness waiting to gather
spirits for the journey to After
where Before is over
and Being becomes the Now of eternity
that knows only whole
...and holy.

Death is not as cruel as Life can be.
It is Love's angel, knowing what awaits,
letting Life have its way
to a journey's turning.
Dying is a part of Life
and can be painfully cruel,
while Death's other name is Peace
and is its own being,
waiting for the moment Life lets go,
while Death itself, gently,
Oh, so gently
lifts each spirit
into the Now of eternal Love.

"If we really think that home is elsewhere and that this life is 'a wandering to find home,' why should we not look forward to the arrival?"

- C.S. Lewis

To a Loved One Dying

You are almost beyond reach -
but for your eyes
when they open to the light
and find us standing by your bed,
telling you it's alright to go,
to step not away from
but into the fullness of being,
into the forever of our hearts.

> *Our eyes speak our love,*
> *see the "Love you's" and the "Thank you's"*
> *on your pale, dry lips.*
> *Our hands feel the fading warmth*
> *on your brow while smoothing hair,*
> *caressing your curiosity*
> *while your eyes blink wonderings.*

There is no pain in us
but that of loss
and wanting more of time
and you.
We make the hours long,
holding on
to what is left
...and leaving.

> *Too soon our hearts will catch*
> *your gasping, fragile, final breath,*
> *then pray Amens to God,*
> *knowing you are home and whole...*
> *while we are left to weep.*

"Dying? Not the end of everything. We think it is. But what happens on earth is only the beginning."

- Mitch Albom

Eden, After

Some nowhere-everywhere,
beyond before and in eternity
when space and time
become unnecessary,
and Now reclaims its purity,
Love's wisdom
envelopes all of everything
and wholeness is home.
Language returns to spirit;
knowing need not question
and will is selflessly instant.

> *In Eden-bliss*
> *imagination becomes itself,*
> *with dreams, as soothing as rainbows,*
> *painting and telling only truth.*
> *The senses of long, long-lost ago's*
> *are one and the same,*
> *full to ever-overflowing;*
> *feelings sing symphonies to themselves*
> *and the embrace of Love*
> *has become the sun.*

In Eden, after,
spirit is Being;
Becoming, unremembered journeys.
Presence is always,
sin has no need for naming.
Silence hums, like distant star-shine,
around, within and through
librettos of Oneness,
the ever, ever hymn
of creation's prodigals;
"We are home; we are whole;
we, the children of Love's wisdom,
finally and quite simply are."

"End? No, the journey doesn't end here. Death is just another path, one we all must take. The grey rain-curtain of this world rolls back, and all turns to silver glass, and then you see it."

- J. R. Tolkien

Getting There

Whoa-ho-ho, what's this? Wha-da-hey!
I'm...I'm gone; left it all behind...
Just like that?
Where the hell am I?
I think...I think I'm somewhere between Then and Now.
"Now?"
Is that the right word? Don't know.
What does Now mean, in this place?
No...space!
No...whatever...

An out-of-body experience?
Or is this the real deal?
Strange. Not dark, not bright.

Just...misty...fuzzy...flat. I shout...something... but
there's no sound. Am floating. Falling? No. Not even
moving. I see without seeing, my hearing a vacuum of
silence. No feelings anywhere. Not even numb.

What? Where? How?

I don't have to turn to know what's around me. It's
like...like...I'm a part of the whole. But...what whole?
Alone. And waiting. But not like there's time passing, or
a line I'm at the end of. And no anxiety. Only a kind
of...peace? A kind of...love?

I think I'm smiling but can't tell. "Hey, what's up? This
some kind of joke? You putting me on?"

Nothing. But I'm fine with that.

Waiting... it's like...like I'm in the middle of a shoreless pond but...there's no water, no boat under me. I yell a soundless "Hello-o-o-o?" into emptiness.

All around, nothing but me, awake, wide awake...and wondering. And still, no anxiety.

Just... quiet questions.

I miss my body. Where is it?

I'm not naked but I think I am, body or no.

Weird. Like...like I'm simply and basically me!

All energy, no form.

Kinda like a snowflake without crystals.

Strange doesn't say it. Nothing does.

But...there's more than nothing.

I just have no name for it.

Memories? Just out of reach. All seems misty ...fuzzy...flat.

Still, it feels like I've been here before, a lifetime ago.

Something stirs around me, like a cashmere cloud, I think. An aura forms an opening in the emptiness. Inviting. Seducing my curiosity. There's more of a push than a pull as I drift toward the opening. I'm like a mote of dust caught in a thread of light, floating free and helpless toward whatever is in, on the other side of the opening. Hopeful. Somehow knowing all the answers await there. Not a tic of anxiety. I nod acceptance.

Finally, and oh so gently, the aura enfolds me with certainty and, in an instant, I sense a feeling of being...home.

Words For a Funeral

(to be spoken slowly, intimately)

Shhh... Listen... Listen...

Can you hear the silence of me? Not in the words being spoken but in the spaces between. In the silence of my being with you.

Can you hear me?

I hear what your hearts are saying but I am too much at peace to weep. I am home, finally, and whole.

Can you sense the truth of that in the silences between these words?

There is no need for language where I am. Love is all there is; It is the energy that unites us, that is eternal.

Can you sense it, feel it in this moment of gratitude, of knowing that love never dies. Bodies do but never the spirit, the energy that unites us.

Where there is love, there is new life, always. Now I know the truth of that; I no longer need to just believe.

Can you hear me in the silences in your hearts?

Your being here, your love for me
is so much of the peace I know and feel –
and want to share.
Shhh... Listen... Listen...
Can you hear my love for you?

A Word After...

Death does not diminish those of us left behind. Rather, it intensifies the awareness of our mortality while reminding us of the wholeness we all seek, motivating us to try to solve the mystery of our meaning. Those who pass on are forever a part of our story, as we are of theirs.

We share a journey of the spirit, a spirit that is eternal, though the journey itself is time-bound. Perhaps that is why death is meant to remind us in our human experience of where we came from and, in our not-knowing, where we are going: Home, where the spirit lives, eternal, whole, and holy.

"In my end is my beginning."

- Mary, Queen of Scots

CPSIA information can be obtained
at www.ICGtesting.com
Printed in the USA
LVHW020841101120
671256LV00008B/273